Where Foxes Roam

Prince Edward Island and Panmure Island

Second Edition

Written by Ann Marie Tomlins

Illustrated by Hailey McCarthy

Where Foxes Roam: 2nd ed Copyright 2019 By Ann Marie Tomlins

All rights reserved. No part of this book may be reproduced in any form by any electronic or mechanical means, including photocopying, recording or information storage and retrieval without permission in writing from the author

ISBN 978-1-987852-19-6

Author: Ann Marie Tomlins: email: annmarietomlins@live.com

Illustrator: Hailey McCarthy; hailey_mccarthy@hotmail.com

Additional copies may be obtained from the author or may be ordered through www.amazon.com

Forward

This story is a tribute to our ancestors, both mine and the foxes. There once was a fox farm on Panmure Island, and the foxes still roam on this beautiful island, where their ancestors used to be.

My ancestors, the Panmure Island and Georgetown MacDonalds, once lived on the island, where they owned a large parcel of land. On a portion of that land now stands the Panmure Island Lighthouse, tall and majestic, on the eastern shore of Prince Edward Island.

The Panmure Island Lighthouse is owned and operated by a community of volunteers, who want to preserve the history of this historical piece of paradise.

I would like to thank the lighthouse volunteers for their support and encouragement in making this book become a reality. I would also like to thank my brother Cyril (C.Y.) MacDonald) for help with editing, my publisher, Tom Schultz, and of course my talented and creative illustrator, Hailey McCarthy.

Ann Marie (MacDonald) Tomlins

Meet the Author

Ann Marie Tomlins is a former Special Education Resource Teacher and Reading Specialist who returned to her beloved Prince Edward Island after retiring in 2010. While teaching, Ann Marie had the privilege of sharing her love of poetry with hundreds of children, who enthusiastically listened to her stories about animals that embark on adventures, face adversity or struggle with being different. Ann Marie's first children's book, *Louie the Looney Loon*, was published in 2016. Her second book, *Leopold the Lion*, was published in 2017. *Where Foxes Roam* is the third in the series. Children will enjoy the simplicity of text and rhyming pattern that helps them read with ease as they view delightful illustrations of foxes as they roam across their beloved island.

Meet the Illustrator

Hailey McCarthy is a self taught, freelance illustrator who lives in Cambridge, PEI. She illustrates in the mornings before her full-time job at Pizza Delight in Montague. This is her fourth children's book; the first book was *Donkey Oatie's Irish Visitor*, written by Tom Rath; her second book was *Leopold the Lion*, also written by Ann Marie Tomlins. Her third book was *Nature Girl* by C.Y. MacDonald. All of Hailey's illustrations are done by free-hand sketch coloured by felt markers. The illustrations in *Where Foxes Roam* have been digitally enhanced to ensure quality, and are sure to delight children of all ages.

On the Eastern coast of Canada,
there`s an island by the sea,
full of friendly, playful foxes,
wild and running free.

It is Prince Edward Island,
the gentle province where
the foxes run so freely,
without worry, without care.

In the autumn you may see them sleeping on some bales of hay;

Or watching as the farmers pack the bales and drive away.

In the winter you can watch them tunnel through the drifts of snow;

Or sliding down the hillside,
as their playmates watch below.

In the spring you see them sunning,
underneath their favorite tree;
surrounded by their babies,
who are cute as cute can be.

Friendly foxes like to travel
to the spots they love the most:
Green Gables, and the beaches
all along the island coast.

At Panmure Island Lighthouse,
you can watch them resting there;
sunning on the picnic tables,
lazing on the big red chair.

It`s the oldest wooden lighthouse,
part of Island History.

The foxes like to be there,
where their papas used to be.

When children build sand castles
with their shovels and their spoons;

The foxes like to watch them from high, up on the dunes.

The shyer ones will hide within
the long green reeds of grass;
sometimes they will sneak a peek,
as if they`re playing hide and seek.

As dusk draws near, they will gather, picking shells and digging clams.

They`ll even look for sea glass,
hidden deep within the sand.

When they`re finished gathering treasures,
and they`re far too tired to roam;
they`ll head for Panmure Island Lighthouse,
the place that they call home.

www.ingramcontent.com/pod-product-compliance
Lightning Source LLC
Chambersburg PA
CBHW061115070526
44583CB00027B/3305